MW00478959

AQUAMARINE

Valerie Duff

LILY POETRY REVIEW BOOKS

Published by Lily Poetry Review Books
223 Winter Street
Whitman, MA 02382

https://lilypoetryreview.blog/

ISBN: 978-1-957755-25-0

Cover photograph: Kikki Ghezzi

Table of Contents

I saw the danger, yet I walked along the enchanted way,
And I said, let grief be a fallen leaf at the dawning of the day.

—Patrick Kavanagh

Who knows how long I've loved you
You know I love you still
Will I wait a lonely lifetime
If you want me to, I will

—The Beatles

for Ernest Arthur and Barbara

for North and Marlowe

I.

Music of the Spheres

On my birthday, I attended
a performance of Bach's fugue in *una chiesa*,
my phrasebook my pikestaff. The organ

shook trains from Venice to Salerno.
I staggered out, an accordion, wondering
how to make a compound sentence,

where *gelati*, where some money,
why the best phrase I could muster
in Italy was: *mi lasci in pace*,

then wandered the *Museo Galileo*'s giant hall
of mechanical devices, repeating to myself,
Museo. Galileo. The building's front,

a Medici fort, stood close to the water.
Inside were complex systems, cogwheels,
barometers, disks, simple microscopes,

telescopes like lifeboats on the walls.
Later, in the hall of the Uffizi,
I stood face to face with The Annunciation,

Gothic art of Memmi and Martini,
in thrusts of brilliant gold
the angel and the virgin (which is which?)

locked in gilded mist between his fingers and her chador-
robe. The self-preserving curl of Mary's shoulders
denies all physics. My heart lifted

to the lily's bright leaf.
The displeased fire lens of her gaze
said *so much more is ahead.*

Then I wept, hardly knowing I was standing
with anyone but the saints, in their exclusive panels,
their stares the still twin eyes of storms.

Biome

There was a blue drink on the porch sill at the Black Whale.

So many things show up on tests.
This is how we live, adjusting odds,

percentages in our favor. Still
I sweated in a hot back room, windows seamed shut

googling survive googling fear,
never death, never radial

symmetry or prime mover, the WiFi ghosting.
Meanwhile outside, bumper cars

and sand toys nested in the oyster grass.
Island birds pieced songs from soft white sand

and little tar not far from Three Mile Island,
the guard who held me upside down.

How close lifeguard to diagnostic tool. I never felt the thing,
the jelly luminescent in my breast. Its Medusa stalks

a wave of supplication, umbrella pulse of dreams.

Full Fathom

five my father hears the island language no one but he can understand, moon sound
     birthed as pearls
that wash up on the shore, hopelandic, split by wind and salt, to fabricate
with quartz and calcium, a colony beneath the sea deep inside the coral boy who has
     my daddy's eyes, and mine,
blue waters stripped from Lake Louise, west Canada, so far from here or Iceland's
     placid touchdown, wave through reef.

My Mother's Route

Virginia lanes, wild blackberry
my mother walked with friends

clusters of green
light wind against her face

the birds telegraph endlessly
a cardinal flickers near the track

mosquito bowls from last night's rain
spill iron mud

four deer running cannot recollect
desire to retrace her

circulates a vine through the gravel
through the soup of honeysuckle

an envelope, as silken as
their love letters no one can see

Wild Nights

—"might I but moor" —Emily Dickinson

I.

The driveway led to papers she could read. She had
a house, a window out, a covered porch.

Two oaks sickened with blight. The rest

strove to crown, their branches wild in storms. These residential
roads she walked with him at dusk, the couple, elderly.

The curbs held anthills and some fungi. Fireflies.

She knew the yard, the bits of cloud, the places where the grass had died.
Wind blew away her marriage nest.

Leaves fell down. Twigs dropped down

and every day she picked them up.
Snow shone down, and she stayed in. Then it was spring.

The magnolia bloomed opulently without him.

II.

She cut the shrubs and swept the brick. She moved the houseplants
from the sun. Outside, crocus, then azalea, daffodils.

She might have pinned them to her side if she'd been warned

they'd all be left behind. She knew the house. She thinks she knows
your name. She's hatched

to elsewhere: who she loved is gone, a house she can't see clearly.

The weather here is fierce. Hear,
make out the silhouettes that thump

her standard elocution now in ribbons

Whose hands are these?
She saw them on her mother once, before she flew away.

The Harvesters

—after Pieter Brueghel

A tree sustains the harvesters' clean whites
so far from town.
Like fountains, water drops of grass heads.
Like postscript, endless roads through Flanders.
Close up, men like lapel buttons

through haloes, mending gold.
The maze leads, panoramic,
to the earth's shelf
and two patrolling birds' small forms
like masters, thrushes out to play.

Each bundle laid for grave, each harvester
asymmetric to a chrome haystack
staggered into silence (I can hope)
by a thrush whose throaty bone work
amplifies an eagerness for lunch.

The workers whittle out their ground.
Branches shade the bread slicer.
Another sprawls
with embryonic warmth across
his weathered face
beside the trunk, life force shot

from the navel of the earth.
In the town outside the town,
haystacks like the legs
of the new world.
Even past the distant village, more
exploding wheat. A tiny wagon

carts a block of butter, dense
but cuttable, a dune
to feed the township energized, hungry, small
and faraway—ice skaters on a green.
Past them a backdrop behind a screen,
the leaves a lattice.

Guide

for my daughter

In the Wellesley
Botanic Gardens
the seedlings
spread in rows,
each dirt patch
a minor
fingerscrape,
silent at contact.

Your babyhood
not unlike
this studied cloister,
your brother
within me then, green-
housed as if fruition
or weather
could strike us
in a lie.

You held my hand,
he held dark
matter. I stooped,
a loaded bullwhip set
to fling, Vetruvian,
my arms, yours, and his
ghostly ones imposed,
a spinning windmill.
You nestled in the sail

then broke free,
chattering loudly
hands on trays

not touching stems,
buds, or the leaves'
small shouts of
hallelujah to the light,
to mist, and green
broad rows,

or maybe
to my red knit hat
with yarn flower
I loved
until I lost it.

Report

Oh, honey,
the unspoken life of the body
and the world in which we drink
tea and eat the ruby
seeds that doom us half to hell.
To be so scared
when considering
the afterlife in the sentinel
pot where tea may steep too long.
A riverbed of tannin coats
the way a specimen lines a dish.
The body, its margin
assessment, has forgotten where it came from,
a snow-capped mountain that's left
its origins behind, strata
too deep to feel, layered up
to melting ice. Its axillary
may one day give way
to a deluge that will hide
the dye stained earth, simply
spun to a surface of water,
a change so gradual
most don't feel the slipping
of the shoreline until core
markers are submerged, until
all systems are undone. Because invasion
history of dragon fire
ignites the satellites
that wink and spread across the galaxy
leaving only the suggestion of ourselves,
prognostic rolls of the dice,
the wheel spins to reassess
when a fortune teller
with the tarot comes to discern

the fireworks display.
All has turned to ash, to sack.
Only skin remains,
a cloak that lived the lie so long:
cutaneous tissue with no diagnostic abnormality.

Lace Curtain You Drape Over Every Mirror

Keep that smile
barbed, the wire
the horse leans against.

Birds crack seeds
on the other side of your glass
door. The body, blind, curves

its hedge down paths
through time's narrow microscope.
A clump of cells, narrow threader

juking the ground,
reverberates.
They say it's gone.

It's gone.
Everyone's hands
shifting you gently,

no knowing
not knowing (you know
that now),

their silent nods,
stonecutter precision,
your plea for the tool.

Heroes

Young bodies flee the maxilla
of city underground at dusk.
In the low thrumming of the nearly-empty shuttle

I slide against the transit polymer. On my phone
a new poet is everywhere, easy come, easy go.
I am at eye-level with a window set in stone

where scholars gather in yellow aquarium glow,
at the Institute for Research, grapes and gouda,
spindled banter so removed

from the anxious, who each day look into short
distances of headlights, an empty row of blue,
the shadows of pedestrian traffic, rush hour.

In this transport through Kendall
we are our own guides, the amazing
grace of subway stairs, footfall

call and response, geese
headed south as if we know
the turn of constellations, returning

home above the evergreens
and frozen treads. Here, still on my phone,
I can't stop looking at the video

of my mother with a man who's not my father
in memory care at ninety. I reflect
back to myself a burnt Nordic

traveler in the glass. She has forgotten
I am here but thank you.
Thank you for. A bit

around the eyes.
This stranger's, too,
in rifts and coasts of saga.

Like candlelight
her body mirrors shapes
it took in Havana, Bogotá,

pausing at a party for the diplomatic corps,
not some Florida ward.
Perhaps I'm just imprinting like a gosling

on my mother's voice. Saviors
never disappoint, don't have to be
my father. These champions.

Wanderlust

In the Egyptian café in London,
I drank coffee with men smoking hookah.
Draw in, breathe out.

The cup was small,
The coffee harsh. I had
to catch a train from Marble Arch.

A still point, Byzantine, one star
in a galaxy of trillions,
I had to find my friends.

Who cares what happened?
I moved like a bat, darted, skittered
towards the river. An old lady

inching towards her complex screamed
when I tried to help her with her walker.
It was my life. The rooftops fracture.

If I hadn't jostled the mosaic
maybe I could stop the picture.
Buildings of stirred beach glass.

Cresting sunsets comb
the face, refine the land.
The world goes sad. Like now?

Like now. Even the ancients
felt slips, skips in experience
plotted as mathematical fact.

II.

Flood

Old Burying Ground, Church Street, Cambridge

Thumbed cockeyed through the bus rush,
slates in shrouds of coats flung dark
against that dirty birch gone hunchback,

where the honey locust scrawls
a jigsaw path, loose scripts around the lot,
washing over settlers who came here first,

who said, *we will, of course, we will.*
As when my injured father spoke,
I knew that I should promise anything,

take boats next summer if he liked,
keep our etched plans alive, deny
what misery, then excess we become.

Lights change direction, traffic, orbit.
The only living man who's in this scene,
a post almost, lies homeless near these littered

ancient skiffs that wave a semaphore
of nicks made hourglass and death's head.

Witch Hunt

Air, fire, water, earth

Fire up a gas line cleans the rock
Gusts can move a hearth behind its glass

Fog, smolder, rainfall, dirt

I might feel bad, except I am
In public, ropes unblemished

Breath, ember, pool, ash

Black from the pull of the rip
In my side, I go down, despite how I swim

Vortex, strata, breaker, flames

The feel of sand in hair, silt
Gives sense of it: stingray passing

Sky, woods, marsh, spark

Sent scattershot to land,
Ripple lacerating past the mad

Blast, soil, spray, blaze

Weight, split the day, coax me back
To test my luck and face the water down

Windmill, totem, furnace, dew

Arrowhead

Melville's monsters of the sea arrive
on balsam tides. Unanchored shale
becomes white whales that clink like shells,
whose fir fronds harbor sisters, cut their Berkshire
ships to splinters, point out finger
rings for all to see, the brazenness of lean-to.
No evidence of whaling but in weaponry
thrown overboard, small and dire, beyond
the fireplace that warmed each floor, dark desk
of glacial spruce whose print seeks wilderness.

King Street

*—in Downtown Boston after the reading of the Declaration of
Independence, King Street turned into State Street. Prison Lane
later became Court Street.*

The frost delayed bog onion.
Cape Cod an ancient brow,

wild and everywhere
sailors crossed, passengers tracked

through jetty moss, replaced *Shawmut*
with *Massachusetts*, thrived.

Old seaweed paths from waterways
wrapped in cheat

fueled the white merchant,
the wide rim of the harbor's

ivory foam. The Charles
roughed out an ice shelf.

Snow fell and fell and fell.
That next summer

when an angry mob decreed
the lion crowned and unicorn with golden horn

had royal prints (easier to have been
a piece of fool's parsley, cut in quarters,

burned through that aphid-ridden summer).
a whipping wind of smoke made blind

workers on the waterfront, cinders in their faces.

Expedition

Before Louisiana, Jefferson signaled Lewis with a mirror to his home at Monticello,

the hilly path between plantations ten miles on horseback. Distance was a summons to expand the language of one's purchase, to annotate direction. Knowing the terrain was, for many, second nature.

Lewis tracked veiny rust-colored routes that arced like hipbones in his drawings. Hazards surfaced. Fallow tradeposts. Weather changed and rivers flooded out, despite the compass. Names now commonplace had meaning.

Do not doubt the frontier is a gift, the explorer might have said. A seedling of topography can tie us tight, comfort us with contour as we feel across an area in which we are so small. But it was the sea we were after.

Aquamarine

News came to me by slow boat;

                        the child

on a steamer
through persimmon curtains, slept away her infancy.
Waves specked the day-bed where she dreamt

                               her mother's best

tight leather, guessed its shift below the tongue.
A parchment-stuck religion, two-in-one.

                            No ocean

trinity for us. Water heaved and dimpled to reveal
a blue eye full of greed, her whale
astonishment and frail,

                              wet anarchy.

Adult Cradle, circa 1800

Against these walls, too thin, a
wooden giant leans. In dimness
we mistake it for a chrysalis.
We rock myths in the cradle.

Fire crackles in the hearth
as snowstorms pit the panes. Nearby, babies
sleep in miniature, with a hood
and crescent moon, while this container's

spindles hook to gasp—wish—canopy
left off reveals interior and injury.
Release the platform from its ring, consecrate
the boards with body, warm, immobile.

The rocker, Shaker-made, allows the parent
to be seen by flame, a small winged form
beneath sheet or bedclothes,
growing smaller.

Reflection

We track mapless.
Hear the bird-calls.

They reply to pressure,
Boot phosphor,

Still ponds. My son,

You and I are
Spruce fall.

We fit beneath
The dripping canopy

Notch the needle

Bed beneath our feet.
Rain-stripped stumps

Reflect the planets

We can't see.
Take on faith

Existence, rings

Aligned to deep, wrenching,
Muddy mitochondria,

Powerhouse of fern

And net, open
On all sides, lowing frogs

And in the pond, the sky.

Chemo: That Open to the Sun

His father lifts him

godlike toxins *make*
him different, make him
live again. World
of grit and dissent

the sun god's son
in phosphorescent veils
of firestream, intravenous
alchemy, permits the shock
the blitz to bring him home.

His eyes shoot through gold
crowds, to marble
columns, base turned lustrous
solid in his hands.
He benefits, then burns.

Immortal
horses near the broken chariot
put out light.
In Phaeton's iron mask,
their still points form.

Pegasus

Iron mallet, shield of glass. Our
genesis a crucible of gas
and condensation shot straight through the aorta
that took on color, luster, gorgon dreds
when one of us reversed and sampled godhead.
To be a wilderness, unstable viable
Medusa spawned right there, shut down
to rock and filled the holding chamber.
Pulled particles developed mass, insisted on
a stallion's eye from iodine and salt, and spat
out cracks, and lonely, spat out code.
It arced from her decapitated neck.
Her hair knot slipped, a heart began to beat.
His hard wings shook like candles.

Folk Magic

We are following the hearse,
the body in the hearse steady
as a tree *not my father*
any longer jagged timber

skidded from the world.
Winter face, eyes tight, reject
the earth. Ground, rough out
Arabian night, let him drown

in trunk and sap. Hoofbeats
hover on the chintz.
Hands, upend the seamless
flying carpet. Wagon

that's been rigged to bear
sharp wind, brace
for final shift. Put your faith in
blue hydrangea ground to powder.

Heat Lightning

Sweat and eucalyptus smell of horses
I imagine once were stabled near tomatoes
tied to posts, still green, blows in. Grass
mowed sharp around the pump that watered it.
Birds sing *there over there* while mountain tops
stand sentinel, the goldfish in the pond.
Some calls I can't identify and some
I can: woodpecker, towhee, crow.
Blue Ridge flutters pine to shrug them off.
The backyard canvas made of hemp
whips wind, a thoroughbred
who canters, counterpoint against the dove,
the outcast in the woods who proves most blue.

Calling

In Memoriam: Seamus Heaney

I.

On my bus route down the Navan Road
we wound our way to the quays.
We were crossing fields of history,
the immigrants who rode with me to work
to clean hotels and chandeliers or wait
and wait by Georgian fronts for papers.

II.

I slept in my wool sweater
by the fireplace with spiders.
It was like you never left,
and yet—you quarried something out,

something marble.
Despite the smoke and damp,
I would have stayed local
legend-like: *Stoneybatter*
Sandymount Howth

III.

When we first met, you were an elegant
windmill, tufts of white hair a thistle's
wispy seeds. I thought of you at Harvard
all my turbulent Dublin year
when I'd buy a cappuccino, sit
the café's posh seat by the glass,
wonder if I'd see you on a corner,
in a bookstore's airless papers,
dog-eared glossy covers.

IV.

You were no doubt, by then, dreaming
Kerry coastlines, lilts of Armagh,
horse chestnuts in the park
where you now
face Yeats, your weighted
radius from the Irish Sea
and the colleagues
to whom you were calling.

III.

Fry's Spring Filling Station

I am sitting in a station
built in the Depression,
an island in a scrap drive sea.
Now they've converted, serve
fire-roasted vegetables,
plates of bread. In the thirties,

home to hobos,
Ford-mint autos, kids
play hide-and-seek by the garage.
In the face of tight-fisted
existence, it saved us all?

Centrifuge of sump,
now it's Roman arches,
columned stones, red brick
and tin, a roof of Spanish shingle.
Neighborhood of nothing

in a mishmash of design
while somewhere else, Fry's wellspring
brims ample, alloy-rich.
Through speakers, Beatles
sing to every diner
and ghosts of vagrants near the dumpster:

I've got no car and it's breaking
my heart Under vines
of white lights
through groundwater, generations
spilling out.

Up Vinegar Hill

Like shafts of hair, moss vines whip across the eye.

Heat unclasps a fan, blowing oaks
and stilling flash to flash. Humidity increases in the grass,

not dew, not damp, but crystalline.
One tap sets it ringing.

Small nesters bark into oblivion. Birdsong:
a million doors squeak on

a million hinges. Then,
the hill is stopped, the sting makes feeling disappear.

Travelers wonder which is ground
(or who is buried where); walking in a dream, one hears

them say "I died in fire," one hears the birds again, one hears
"conception proved difficult," split and held apart like oil.

John Kerry's Concession Speech

Faneuil Hall, 2004

Some of us, as Adam's mindless fart
shapes the head of a pin, knew enough
to hear him speak, the words' repeated strike,
as from an heirloom clock,
makes the body's fall to pavement more bearable.
A crowd, we had no entry
but through stillness, willed to scaffold the building.

Where was he? In a backroom carving chickens
from a block of wood, practicing the speech
we could understand: the train
was to be full. Red, white, and blue
washed each hand, streamers wrapped in a vain show

against the last months, pressed a vein
on his head, seaming his brow
while we clapped and screamed a shower
of bullets, partly because we were caught in the vision,
partly because we were cold.

We revelers, now numb,
had to go back to work (we all had work).
The candidates dispersed
but a name there stayed long after, a leaf
furled to the tree with those white
leaders, asking how lost,
how far down.

Water Disco

It blinds—the asphalt nightclub's

thrum and vapor. A backward glance,

   I-29 all steam and water stippled down a windshield.

   Outside, oak leaves decompose. There's too much
noise,

light drawls I can't unhinge. In dark,

cicadas cease, from parchment shelters,

   trilling from a kudzu wall.

   Rain rings the car roof, falls

in beaded curtains through the back door of my vision.

Streets, glossed and igneous, spilling buttons.

Anatomy

The stripping taught mechanics—
one even had kittens inside.
A girl burst into tears (she'd left
to pull apart a bivalve) when cohorts
hoisted patchwork furs, fake meows
beneath the puppetry (childhood's
adage for undressing, *skin the cat*,

chilly and precise). I will never see
a cat the same again, one student said.
His eyes, by then, bedeviled.
All week the college guessed
formaldehyde, lab allergies,
some Egyptian feline's
wrath, some psyche maimed.

We carved out pieces of the pet
(icy hard, yet labile) lengthened
the intestine, stroked the heart,
slit the lungs like two shelled peas.
When at last that student sat, corneas
explored in hospital, the doctor's light
produced a set of stars, a galaxy
behind the lids. Webs of vessels

spread their shadows, sprinkled lines
like whiskers. When the nurses flushed them
with cool water, irritation was relieved.
At once, he knew the simple machine
cat is, who cries and flinches,
frantic, sinks its teeth
into the circuitry of other species.

Doing What They're Told

That kid appears a burned
bright volta, sparkling stone.

Hot pokers, steamed imagination,
hers fill with grown-up voices:
can do better. No one placates steam,

and she sprints through it, clocks
a marathon to gate where boy is

waiting. These critiques will scorch you.
What's in a name? Nurse slaps
her strange applause, her cold fish opera,

back and forth, in drift-net hues,
while those two do what bodies tell them to.

My Exit

I could have been from Glasgow,
the green sign says. It points
across the Blue Ridge,

names Lynchburg and Natural Bridge.

I could have been from Early Street
but it lay on the wrong side,
inner defenses having divided

the fort Black from White.

I might have had my birth at Peaks
of Otter, but all the beasts
were trapped for pelt and meat,

the Lodge shut down and sold.

I always wish I'd been from Ivy
where the sunlight meets the trees
and the speckled shadows ripple

from the red clay to the creek.

Legacy

patched in a box, tidal
pool of tape and glue
her 1914 children's books,
one orange-checkered
cover, relic
tablecloth or flag
spread empty remnants
of belonging this book starts
with boy in four-post bed
tell me

the story, the book
was *watermelon*
pete, the neighbor was
an old white man
and there was theft
of watermelon
the neighbor, known,
gnarled, the book
so old

I hear a train
going somewhere
in the distance, the beat
of its wheels along the track
calls to pete
who doesn't know
just who he is
the need to take
page to page, gave
the watermelon back
to that old man, despite

the fact he reaped for him
along that track
blood ties of soil and stems
the neighbor man and pete
while pete's kin
till and plow their skin
across the field, pulsing hard
like the train, from the crop
as the old man locks watermelon in his bin

Hurricane

Stirring instant coffee, I ask you if you've read
The Day They Shook the Plum Tree, knew islanders
who drank grandfather's gin, sponged out his extra-dry
martini's olive buoy, hung lamps, glass thick as pine.

The wind's a strung-out heirloom, whips by Engleside,
its trumpet blasting: *where'd you get*
those eyes? Broadcast static, creak of wicker,
water's edge unfastens. Then the sea

from salt-box to pavilion, Fifth and Beach,
where ships, unmoored,
waked and rolled before big storms, big wars.

Titanic

Go down steam
punk, dead weight
in water, steam trunk
loose on the cold
warped deck.

Press tight
this way, the ship's
jammed metal fist
against a wind-
whipped shawl, in pieces, no
mouth

left, glory
one hand
print burned
on a hull's brittle rivets. Coffin-
safe passage, dock & bow,
raft & ice,

all you held
dear, your
beautiful beautifully
          wrecked.

Gentrified

The coffee's good, but I wonder where those people

I used to see on porches have gone,
leaning over railings in the heat, the state

of their homes. Is the living Jesus on the wall?

Does their roof still leak? Their junk heap
is not *join you for dinner*.

My roommate had a tick

like concrete in her shoulder.
I couldn't identify it for her.

It could have been a nevus on her skin.

She had it scooped out, she pantomimed
how the doctor dug and dug, bigger than it looked

when she raised her shirt

in the sunlight and begged
me, someone she had known a day,

to check. She knows her body,

she said. Some nights I startle from sleep,
wonder what it is I haven't done

that must be done, what pill

I didn't take, what one thing
could make a difference I forgot.

What mistake I will make next.

My roommate has a course of drugs to take.
I look for ticks on the surface

of my skin, I check exposed arms,

back of my knees, I feel over the scar
because there is no feeling there

a tick could make, the new breast shape

a badge that makes me happy,
my war wound, a permanent limp.

I want to be a small

spot on moving earth that doesn't recognize me,
moss growth my initials forever

in the trunk of a tree, so many ferns and roots

waiting to be freed,
back and forth I go across the James

and am a taxidermist's dream.

Iceland

Here come the boats from Denmark,
Here come the boats from Norway,
from the endless stretch of nothing
to the island jaunt of nothing.

Cliffs a million campsite fires.
Farms few and far between
as under kitchen light, misty blue,
geothermal water fills with sulfur.

Sheer velocity against my face
no matter where I turn
my little horse against the wind.
There goes our boat to Ireland.

From endless solstice light
to magma chambers spilled and cold,
the wind eats everything.
We shelter by a hill.

The Story of the Blue Ridge Mountain Boxwood

Saplings in a coldtruck shimmy back and forth through diesel,

whiffs of rotted ivy   to the mansion looking empty,
lacking border, where it oversees brown water. Windows glint
medicinal green lettering :: *Virginia Boxwood Company* ::
graphic banner stenciled on the van. Unscrambled, shrubs then flank

astonishing blue range. Small birds shit from them.
Boxwoods thrive on mountaintop or vale
but offer no authority, just cuttings or a partial shade.
After harvest, thimblefuls will multiply and maze.
When thinned, their light   breathes out a cardinal.

For Sale

Before I knew what it meant to be
a collector, to gather keepsakes
by the windows acorns pelt like kisses
have them always (little wild things.
Pick them from the baked Virginia brick
closed off and August hot),
I stacked the mirrors, desks, clocks

on which I built my moving pyramid,
the Evesham, Wedgwood, Spode.
Off the ripple of a cup, motif
of trumpet vine, I scaled the roof,
camellia-shaded, stained, looted
riot green. Through jackknifed scents
of moss and rain, I stopped to watch between

the shutters. Escape on slate
where once I dropped the blessed
porcelain, harvested and swept
shard Lear, shard daughter
toward balusters, the house
steeped in light so green (botanic,
blossomed, source unknown).
I blow the fine-grain kingdom
through my fingers, won't
again, or change the locks, or fix you up
in case someone comes to the door.

Acknowledgments

Thank you to Dan Beachy-Quick, Cheryl Follon, Jennifer Barber, Jacqueline Pope, Meg Tyler, Daniel Pritchard, Beth Woodcome Platow, Lynne Potts, and Leslie Williams for looking at drafts. Gratitude for the poetic sensibilities and friendship of the late Leslie McGrath. Thanks to the Writers' Room of Boston and VCCA, where many of the poems came into being. To Drs. Partridge, Golshan, Harris, and Hergrueter at Dana Farber for keeping me here to write these. Thanks to Remy Holzer Kirsch, always my primal reader. To Jake Strautmann, for your deep belief in the sea we were after. To Northanna, my aquamarine, and to Marlowe, my reflection—you are indeed the poems themselves.

To the following editors, thanks for including work in this or slightly different form from this book in your publications: John Hennessey, *The Common*; Don Share, *POETRY;* Danielle Legros Georges and Ben Berman, *Solstice*; Peter Campion, *Great River Review*, Michael Simms, *Vox Populi*, Jennifer Barber and Fred Marchant, *Salamander*; Adam Piette and Alex Houen, *Blackbox Manifold,* Sven Birkerts and Bill Pierce, *AGNI; Noon*; Jennifer Martelli, Marjorie Tesser, *Mom Egg Review*; Jennifer Lowe, *Gulf Coast* (online exclusive); Kevin Gallagher, *SpoKe*; Ginger Murchison, *The Cortland Review*; Anne Brechin, *Prague Revue*; James Byrne, *The Wolf*; Jessie Lendennie, *Salmon Poetry 35th Anniversary Anthology*. Thank you, Eileen Cleary, for giving this book a home with Lily Poetry.

About the author

Valerie Duff has held fellowships from the VCCA and Writers'
Room of Boston. Her first book, *To the New World* (Salmon Poetry,
2010), was shortlisted for the Seamus Heaney First Collection Poetry
Prize from Queens University, Belfast. She is a freelance writer and
editor, and a coach at Hillside Writing. She is thrilled to be part of
the Lily Poetry family.

CHI
Chy - Chi m (plural treven or chiow), noun: house.
Priest's Cove, Cape Cornwall, UK.

"Enveloping an abandoned stone house nestled under a cliff beside the sea allowed me to reflect upon the perpetual principles of impermanence, repair, and renewal. Using vivid blue fishing net and rope to cover its sides and to weave together the precarious slate pieces of its broken roof, I became a mother bird, each day slowly expanding and repairing my nest when the sea and wind unraveled it. My rhythm was the Moon's dance. I rose when the tide went down, often encountering on the stony beach a fisherman who lived according to the same ancient clock. I worked during low tide, clambering about the structure until the cold salt water had swirled up to cover the rocks on which the old Cornish house sat. The sea, like a true artist, with his unforgiving liquid hands rose up and undid large parts of my work. Nothing survived but the essence, and the mother bird, returning like the tide to continue her work."
(Kikki Ghezzi)

Though rooted in drawing and painting my work often includes various experimental forms – installations, sculptures, textiles and artist's books. What matters most is a fading into a more impersonal process, a love and affection for the language and materials in which and from which the object is revealed, the oneness between the made and maker. As the ego begins to dissolve in presence, 'the picture draws the picture', 'the fabric weaves the fabric', 'the color paints the color'. Kikki Ghezzi's work has been exhibited internationally and is part of private and public collections including the Institute of Fine Arts of NYU NY, Museo San Fedele Milano, MuSa, La Civica Raccolta del Disegno Museo di Salo' Italy, Villa Firenze and the Italian Embassy Washington D.C., Museo Giuseppe Sciortino Palermo Italy, The National Museum of Women in the Arts Washington D.C.

Printed in the USA
CPSIA information can be obtained
at www.ICGtesting.com
LVHW040805060923
757193LV00006B/141